Gerbil Basics: How

rbil

ISBN-13: 978-147751780
ISBN-10: 1477517804

Copyright Notice

GERBIL BASICS

How to Buy and Care for a Pet Gerbil

May Tenston

I dedicate this book to every person – be they man, woman or child that has been lucky enough to have their lives touched by the joy, excitement and sheer abundant love a gerbil can bring every day. May it long continue.

Contents

Gerbils
An Introduction

Highly intelligent, curious, energetic and cute.

These adorable animals have a loveable personality and make the ideal pet for people of all ages.

They love to search everything around them and are naturally inquisitive.

If you watch a gerbil for a few minutes it can be exhausting. You would think all that scurrying, sniffing and investigating would tire them out. But they have boundless energy and are a joy to watch.

They don't keep still for very long as they are always climbing, sniffing, running and investigating everything around them with a fearless nature.

Chewing machines

One of the gerbil's major characters is their insatiable appetite for chewing. Give them a new toy and they immediately want to chew it. This natural tendency to chew everything in sight comes from millions of years of inherited behaviour.

In the wild they must scratch, chew and explore their surroundings to seek out food. Their very survival depends on it.
So be warned. Whatever you give them they will try to chew. Make sure to only give them toys and objects specially designed to be safe for gerbils to chew. Your local pet shop should be able to advise you.

Curious and cute

Gerbils love to investigate everything around them. Their in-built inquisitive nature makes them want to seek out new experiences, objects, and of course food.

They can be seen doing this in the wild, so when brought into captivity they continue displaying this behaviour and will happily explore their cage for hours. Being fiercely territorial they scent mark their cage and will defend their home against any potential threats.

Clean creatures

Throughout the daytime gerbils like to groom themselves by licking their paws and rubbing their fur in a stroking motion.
While very cute to watch this is an important ritual for gerbils as they love to stay clean at all times.

So why then do they like to bathe in sand?
Well at first this may seem like a contradiction. After all they like to keep clean so why would they want to get all dirty again? Well, taking a sand bath helps remove excessive oil and residue that can build up under a gerbil's fur.

In the beginning

The term "gerbil" is derived from the Latin word "gerbillus," which means "little jerboa."
The term "jerboa," in turn, refers to a jumping desert rodent commonly found in the remote regions of Africa and Asia.

Strictly speaking, the jerboa and the gerbil are both non-natives of the Western Hemisphere.
Most of the gerbils kept as pets are Mongolian gerbils, which are natives of Eastern Mongolia and Northeast China.

Tracing the animal kingdom's family tree, you'll realize that true gerbils belong to the order Rodentia and sub-order Myomorpha.

Their super-family is Muroidea and they belong to the family Cricetidae and sub-family Gerbillinae. They're part of the genus Meriones and the species Unguiculatus.

Size

A mature gerbil is a bit larger than a mouse, but smaller than a rat. A gerbil's body is about 10cm long and its furry tail is of the same length. Its weight is typically 115g or less.

Gerbils have either tawny or reddish brown fur on their tail and back, with a gray undercoat and black outer tips. Their belly is either creamy white or light gray. They have shorter ears and broader heads than mice or rats. They also have large dark eyes that slightly bulge, elongated hind legs, and relatively small forefeet.

The general appearance, colour, actions, and postures of a gerbil are similar to those of squirrels and are entirely suitable to life in the desert.

Wild gerbils

Wild gerbils are often referred to as sand rats, desert rats, or jirds and very little information is known about their life.

It's general knowledge, though, that these are burrowing animals typically living far from water sources and living off of grains, seeds, grasses, plants, and roots found in the desert.

They're extremely active during the day and to a lesser extent at night.
A gerbil colony lives inside a tunnel about two to three meters long and with a number of entrances. Their tunnels are typically several meters deep, branching off at different ground levels. There are also several chambers that serve as nesting rooms and food storage areas.

Desirable pets
Gerbils were first studied by scientists during the 1950s and were found to be very gentle and easy to care for. For this reason, they soon were deemed as desirable pets.

Although they're not cuddly creatures, they do enjoy being handled and bite only when mistreated. Children and adults alike are fascinated by the gerbil's friendliness, curiosity, and quick movements that resemble those of a squirrel.

You're also sure to appreciate the fact that gerbils have very simple housing, food, and water needs. They're also odourless and clean, and it's very easy to keep that way.

Furthermore, gerbils hardly make any noise and are relatively healthy and hardy. They neither hibernate during winter nor become lethargic during summer. You can be assured that they won't try to escape and if they do get loose somehow, recapturing them is a relatively easy task.

What you do need to remember is that gerbils are happiest when they're kept with a mate, so you should be prepared to take care of gerbil babies as well.

Another option would be to get a pair of gerbils beyond breeding age. This way, you get to enjoy their friendly behaviour and interesting activities without having to contend with babies.

Behaviour

A huge part of the gerbil's appeal lies in its interesting habits and customs, which are part of its daily life. To enjoy life with your pet better, it's important that you become familiar with their traits and behaviours so you understand them better and are better able to care for them properly.

To start with, you need to understand that a gerbil lives its life in cyclic activity. Throughout the entire day, it alternated between intense activity and short naps.

Awake

Whenever it's awake, the gerbil tends to run to and fro and investigate just about everything it sees in its surroundings. It also continually nibbles on food, makes nests, burrows into bedding, and gnaws on whatever material it finds. It's not difficult to understand why the gerbil needs occasional rest periods throughout the day.

Napping

You'll know your gerbils are preparing for a nap when they start stretching their forefeet and yawning the way a cat or dog does.

Soon enough, they'll be in a sleep so deep you may start wondering if they're still alive. Some gerbils also push away the bedding in warm weather and lie directly on the cage floor. They can sleep curled up, stretched out on their stomach, or flat on their back.

When the weather is cool, gerbils tend to sleep tucked together with their heads between their hind feet and their tails curled around their bodies. Take note that you shouldn't disturb a sleeping gerbil, as that can make them quite irritable.

What's that?

Whenever you approach your gerbils' cage, you can expect them to approach you as well and try to see what new toy or food you have for them.

Gerbils are eager to investigate just about anything you give to them and because they're compulsive chewers, you need to make sure that none of the toys you provide can harm them. Their interest in new things, however, is typically short-lived and they'll soon look for something new to investigate.

But, their curiosity is such that if you place a gerbil inside a maze with food at the finish line, it's sure to explore every nook and cranny of the maze no matter how hungry it is.

When kept in captivity, gerbils are less likely to learn fear from their experience. They may get startled by loud noises or sudden movements, but such a reaction will most likely be born out of surprise instead of fear.

Gerbils are generally unafraid of encountering new faces, strange objects and noises, or other animals. Therefore, you should be very careful about letting your gerbils meet your other pets, as their innate curiosity might cause other animals to hurt them. You should either keep the gerbils away from your other pets or train the other pets to ignore your gerbils.

Burrowing

When left in the wild, gerbils typically spend a considerable time burrowing to search for food and build their homes. They do this by digging quickly with their forefeet and kicking excavated material with their hind legs. They may also push things out of their way using their head.

Gerbils have very sharp nails on their forefeet, which gives them the ability to burrow even through cardboard, plastic, or scratch wood. It's a good thing they're not fond of scratching their owners.
There may be times when you look into a gerbil's cage and think your pet is missing. Chances are great he's just burrowed into the bedding material. A simple rap on the cage will encourage your pet to emerge from its hiding place.

Gnawing

A gerbil's incisors continue growing throughout its entire lifetime and the animal can't survive for very long if it's left too short or too long.
This makes it important for you to provide your gerbils with a block of wood they can use for tooth exercises. Providing them with hard food also helps a lot in keeping their incisors within the ideal length.
Don't be alarmed if you see your gerbils gnawing or attempting to gnaw at just about anything they see around them – wood, bone, cardboard, bedding material – as this is a normal part of their daily lives.

Sounds

Gerbils are generally quiet, which is among the biggest reasons why people like having them as pets. The only vocal sound they make is a faint and high-pitched "sqeek-sqeek" that a bird's cheep. You're only likely to hear some noise from your gerbils if there's a litter and the parents are having some sort of argument.

From the age of weaning, make drumming or thumping sound on the bedding with their hind legs.
This sound is often a warning or a call for attention. It can also indicate excitement at the new surroundings or during mating period. And when a gerbil burrows or scratches at the walls or floor, you'll likely hear a rasping or rustling sound.

Activity

One of the gerbil's most interesting talents is its ability to jump up with its hind legs. This ability has earned the animal the nickname of "pocket kangaroo." Gerbils can start jumping as soon as they're weaned and can jump up to nearly a metre whenever necessary.

When a group of young gerbils are startled, they can resemble a box of jumping beans as they scatter in several directions.

This special ability allows them to jump backwards, forwards, sideways, or turn around in mid-air. Older gerbils don't jump as often as young ones and those held in captivity don't usually jump as high as their counterparts in the wild.

Gerbils typically move about with all four of their feet, although they can pause to stand or sit on their hind legs from time to time. This is the position they usually take when they eat or drink.

When their curiosity is aroused, gerbils tend to stretch upwards and lean slightly back while maintaining balance with their tail.
A gerbil's tail can also act as a rudder to guide it through the air as it jumps. Gerbils can also climb a vertical wire mesh easily, although they can't hang upside-down for too long.

Well-groomed

Gerbils keep themselves well-groomed because they like being clean at all times. They scrub their faces, ears, heads, bodies, and tails using their tongue and forepaws; the action is so much like that of a cat's.

Gerbils also often groom each other not just to promote cleanliness, but also to stimulate their skin, prevent their fur from matting, and help keep their coats glossy. Because they come from arid climates, the skin of gerbils produces its own natural oils that help combat dryness.

Their coats may get ruffled by high humidity and dampness, and gerbils take care of this by rolling in bedding material and grooming themselves.

Choosing a gerbil

A healthy gerbil typically starts leading a full and active life at the age of one month.

However, it's best to get gerbils when they're already about six to eight weeks old just to make sure they're already hardy enough to be taken away from their mothers. Gerbils of this age are also less likely to be nervous and their actions and appearance at this time should already be interesting enough to give you pleasure.

You probably already know that gerbils are happiest when kept in pairs, but you should also make sure the pair you get are of opposing genders. When two females or two males are caged together, they're likely to fight, especially if they come from different families.

If you choose to raise just one gerbil, then you should shower it with attention and keep it active and happy with lots of toys.

What to look out for when buying

Due to their cute features and easy-going nature gerbils make the ideal pet for children. But what do you look for when buying one?

Well its always advisable to purchase your first gerbil from a recognised branded pet store or an established well-known breeder.

Most pet stores stock the most popular gerbil which is the Mongolian gerbil. You can easily recognize it from its brown coat.

When choosing your gerbil speak to the staff in the pet store and ask their advice and assistance on finding the right cage, food and toys to keep your new gerbil healthy and happy.

You could also buy your new gerbil from a local breeder. Be sure to look into the breeder experience and ask them how long they have been breeding gerbils to get an idea of their level of experience. You should be able to find breeders in your local newspaper or community magazine.

You can also find gerbils for sale in your local papers small ads section. But be careful when buying this way as you could end up with a gerbil with poor health if you are not sure what you are doing. And if you do mistakenly buy a sick gerbil it may spread disease to other gerbils that you have, so it's best to avoid buying this way unless you are confident you know what you're doing.

To read more about how to tell if a gerbil is healthy read the 'health' section later in the book.

When you buy gerbils, look for those that move in a quick and bobbing manner similar to a squirrel.
Your gerbils should also be alert; a healthy gerbil is one that's easily startled by sudden movement, so feel free to try this out on a gerbil before buying it. Choose gerbils with firm-looking bodies that are moderately filled out and make sure their furs are long, glossy, and soft.

Furthermore, you need to make sure their heads and noses aren't long or thin and that they have small ears that stand erect and aren't too rounded. They should have relatively large, but not bulging eyes and these eyes should be twinkling and bright.

A gerbil's tail is only about one-fourth the length of its body at birth, but will grow to nearly as long as its body when the animal is full-grown.

This makes it difficult to assess its health through its tail at a young age, but you should look out for stubby tails with blunt tips or for kinks in the gerbil's tail, which can result from injury.

You should also make sure the feet and nails of your chosen gerbils are in good condition and that they don't have scabs on their mouth, partly closed eyes, sore spots on their rumps, or lumps on their nose or head.

Other warning signs you should look for are bald spots that may indicate dietary deficiency, frequent scratching that may signal the presence of external parasites, and disease symptoms like runny nose, wet bottom, sores, and skin ulcerations.

Here are 8 tips to consider when buying a gerbil:

1. Ensure you buy a gerbil that is healthy and that has been kept in a clean cage.

2. Test how healthy the prospective gerbil is by putting your finder into the cage. If the gerbil is healthy it should perk up pretty quickly. If it doesn't this may be a sign of poor or sluggish health.

3. Check their eyes are bright, sparkling and fully open.

4. Ensure their fur is smooth and clean with no thin or rough patches.

5. If you purchase a pair of gerbils make sure they have lived together before, so they are familiar with each other. This will help save you time training them when you get home.

6. Observe your gerbil walking to check for any signs of uneven posture or poor muscle tone.

7. Try to buy a gerbil that is approximately eight weeks old.

8. Check the gerbil's rear legs are clean and free from dirt. If they are dirty or soiled this could be a sign of poor health.

Home from home

When picking a cage gerbil numbers must be kept in mind. Naturally, the more gerbils there are, the bigger the cage required.

There are a number of cages well-suited to gerbils that are offered in most reputable pet shops. These can be made of wire mesh, sheet metal, chew-proof plastic or a combination of any of these materials. Avoid flimsy plastic cages where possible, as gerbils will try to chew through the plastic given the opportunity.

Ventilation is very important for gerbils so make sure whatever design of cage you choose it has enough ventilation to allow the gerbil to breathe when the bedding material is in place. Take note that gerbils thrive best in cages equipped with a solid bottom. For one pair of gerbils and a litter, floor space of about 40x40cm should be adequate.

Your chosen cage should be about 20-25cm high, considering the gerbil's habit of drinking and eating in a seated position.

When choosing a gerbil's cage, be sure to take cleanliness, weight, security, and durability into consideration.

Next, you need to place shelter and toys in the cage.

Time for toys

Gerbils love playing and look playing with, and exploring new toys and objects.

Their curious nature means they will fearlessly investigate almost anything you put in their cage. Just be sure it's safe for them to chew and big enough that they can't swallow small parts, or get their head stuck in! They are very curious after all.

These days most good pet shops stock a variety of gerbil-safe toys and accessories.
One of the all-time favourite accessories is the running wheel. Most gerbils love running around a wheel, and can stay occupied for hours during the day this way. Wheels are also a great way to make sure your gerbil get enough exercise. Ensure the wheel you buy is big enough for the size of gerbil you have and is well constructed and sturdy enough to withstand an occasional chew.

Hide and seek

Gerbils love to hide.

They feel secure and safe when they hide, so it's important to provide them with adequate hiding places they can escape to inside their cage.

You can buy 'hides' at any good pet store. They usually are available in a variety of materials, from wood, to ceramic to chew-proof plastic.

You can also make your own inexpensive home-made hide from an upturned half a coconut shell. It certainly looks great with the hairy shell giving an almost caveman-like look amongst the bedding at the bottom of the cage. Brown paper bags also make a great – if short-lived hide. Gerbils love to gnaw and chew at the paper to tear it up, eventually hiding under it to disappear from sight.

Climbing

Climbing is another activity that gerbils love. So try adding some sturdy accessories inside the cage which they can climb up.

Most pet shops stock mini-ladders, fake boulders, miniature climbing frames, transparent plastic tubing and other items gerbils love to have fun climbing on.

Rolling in the dust

Gerbils love rolling in the sand and dust, so make sure you have an area of the base of the cage covered in some sand.

Or if you prefer you can put a shallow tray or plastic lid with a little sand on top to let them play in. Rolling in the sand is a fun and functional pastime for the gerbil. They love doing it, but it also helps them clean the oil from their coat and keep them clean.

Put a ceramic or wood house in the corner for the gerbil to take shelter. Attach a water bottle with a metal spout to one side of the cage so the gerbil can drink at regular intervals. Also place a ceramic feeding bowl down on one side.

A few chewable toys are also advisable as gerbil love nothing more than having a good chew – as this keeps them happy. Hay, tissue and paper shred bedding is also advised as this can chewed on also.

A little ladder or climbing toy is also advised as gerbils love to climb and this ensures they are intellectually challenged.

Bedding

We all love a comfortable bed, and your gerbil is no different.
One of the simplest ways to keep your gerbil happy is provide with the right bedding. Try to keep the bedding the same, after you clean the cage, as this makes the gerbil feel at home. Remember gerbils whole life revolves around the scent of things, so be careful not to throw out the bedding all at once as this will remove too much of their scent and likely make them upset

Most bedding comes in three later:

1. **The litter at the bottom**
   This is usually made from a mixture of sand and
   s small amount of cat litter (for hygiene purposes
   and help stop viruses spreading) and this layer is
   up to 4cm deep.

2. **Next comes the support bedding**
   This layer keeps down the dirt and helps absorb
   moisture in the cage. It also is great for the gerbil
   to chew on and to practise burrowing!

3. **The top layer of nesting bedding**
   Important for your gerbils comfort this layer is
   used for sleeping and napping in the day. If the
   room where you keep your gerbil is lower than
   70 degrees Fahrenheit then more bedding will be
   needed to keep your gerbil warm. If the room is
   kept at more than 70 degrees Fahrenheit then
   less bedding is needed and an open-topped nest
   can be used to allow air to circulate.

Co-habitation

Gerbils are territorial by nature, and can be very
aggressive to other gerbils they don't know. If you buy
a gerbil and wish to introduce it to one you already
have, try using the split-cage approach. This allows
gerbils to get to know each other scents without them
fighting.

First, buy some fine mesh wire and fix it in place as a divider down the middle of the cage, making sure the corners as secure.

Now you can place one gerbil on each side of the mesh. Keep an eye on them as they may try to burrow under the mesh if it's not securely installed.

Over time the gerbils will become used to each other scent and then you can remove the mesh.

Health

Gerbils usually maintain good health without too much fuss and require little medical attention. This most common health complaint amongst gerbils is an occasional red nose from scratching it on the inside of their cage. If you suspect your gerbil has a sore nose its best to take them to a qualified vet to get checked out. They will prescribe medication – usually a cream or lotion - to help reduce the infection.

Teeth

Missing teeth is another ailment that gerbils are susceptible to from time to time.

Often caused by a deficiency in calcium or an infection, tooth loss can be hard to spot unless you inspect your gerbil's teeth regularly. One obvious sign of potential teeth problems is a sudden decrease in weight or loss of appetite. If tooth loss has been diagnosed by your vet, you may have to grind their food down a little to help them eat it, particularly if they lose a tooth at the front of their mouth.

Scent glands

One of the more serious health problems that can occur with gerbils is tumors on their scent glands. To find the scent gland just look for the bald patch of fur on the gerbil's tummy. Check that this looks normal. If the scent glad looks sore or inflamed then take your gerbil to see the vet.

Liver

Gerbils can sometimes suffer from liver failure. You can recognise this by watching for the following signs:

- Drinking water excessively.

- Sudden loss of weight.

If you recognize any of these signs take your gerbil to the vet as quickly as you can.

Ears

Problems with the ears usually show themselves through symptoms of imbalance. If your gerbil falls over a lot and becomes clumsy this can sometimes be caused by infections in the middle ear. Your vet should be able to take care of it relatively simply by prescribing some antibiotics. This should be clear up the problem in no time.

Flu

If you notice your gerbil having difficulty breathing, then this could be the symptom of respiratory flu. Much like ear infections this can usually be solved by a short course of antibiotics from your vet.

Stroke

Just like humans gerbils can be severely affected by strokes. Symptoms of stroke to look out for include:

- Inability to balance

- Falling over while walking

- Poor co-ordination

If your gerbil shows any of these symptoms take it to the vet immediately.

Dinner time

When you see your gerbils scratching, gnawing, and burrowing, you don't have to be afraid that they're trying to escape from the cage. These are instinctive actions and it's likelier for your gerbils to get out of the cage by accident.

The good thing is that gerbils are often quite eager to return to its home (in this case, the cage), especially if you encourage it with a few sunflower seeds placed near the opening of the cage.

Due to its innate curiosity, it'll probably take its own sweet time exploring the surrounding areas, but it'll soon return to you and the cage as long as you stay still and wait patiently.

Another effective way to recapture an escaped gerbil is to place a plastic tube or cardboard near it and then use bedding or seeds as bait.

This method makes use of the gerbil's natural love for exploring tunnels.

As soon as the gerbil enters the tube, you can easily cover the exits with your hands and return the animal to its cage. An empty container or bucket may also be used for this purpose.

But, more than being concerned that your pets will escape, you should be concerned about maintaining its health and satisfying its energy needs.

This can be done by providing the gerbils with a properly balanced diet.

Food

As with us humans a balanced diet is ideal for your gerbil.

Gerbil food comes in two major categories:

1. Seed mix

2. Block feed

Pet shops normally offer food mixes that are especially formulated to meet your gerbils' dietary requirements.

A typical gerbil mix is comprised of a variety of grains such as:

- Wheat

- Oats

- Barley

- Corn

Peanuts, vegetable flakes, pumpkin, sunflower seeds, and other small seeds may also be included in the mix. This mix forms the bulk of a gerbil's diet.

To supplement this you can give your gerbil occasional treats such as:

- Plain biscuits (dog biscuits can be given also)

- Dry bread

- Fresh fruit or raisins

- Vegetables such as carrots and broccoli.

- Small amounts of cheese

- Breakfast cereal (small amounts at first to see how well they digest it)

The general rule is to feed an adult gerbil a tablespoonful of food each day; young gerbils require only half of that amount.

Feeding routine

While there isn't a strict rule as to when to feed your pet gerbils, it's generally advised to keep to some sort of routine.

You should feed your gerbil approximately every 24 hours, and at roughly the same time every day. The late afternoon or evening is a good time to feed them (maybe after you have your dinner in the evening).

Pretty soon, your pets will get used to the routine and remember when to expect food.

You'll notice them becoming very active when they hear the usual sounds associated with the feeding routine.

Take a note of how much food they each so you can regulate the amount of food you provide so as not to waste unwanted food.

Place the feed in a ceramic or heavy-based bowl. Always make sure to give treats in a separate bowl so this becomes associated with treats in the gerbils mind. You can also hand-feed the gerbil which is a great way to bond with your gerbil and great fun too.

Gerbils don't hoard food and they don't overeat, except where sunflower seeds are concerned. This is their favourite treat and it can be fascinating to watch a gerbil manipulate a sunflower seed in its forepaws, open the shell, devour the kernel, discard the husk, and immediately reach for another seed.

Take note, though, that these seeds contain a significant amount of fat, so be sure not to give too much to your pets.

Vegetables

The dry food you feed your gerbils should be adequately supplemented with green vegetables a few times each week so your pets can get additional vitamins and minerals.

Fresh lettuce, carrots, celery, parsley, kale, apple peel, parsnips, dandelion, alfalfa, and grass should do the trick.
Although gerbils aren't susceptible to diarrhoea, you should still be careful to provide these only in small amounts to avoid intestinal upsets.

Your pets may show their own food preferences and you'll surely enjoy testing their tastes, especially since there's a considerable amount of possible variations where the gerbil diet is concerned. Make sure you provide hay at all times to help with digestion, promote a glossy coat, and serve as bedding material.

Your gerbils' food may be served in a heavy and shallow saucer that can't be easily tipped over. You may also use a food container that can be attached to the side of the cage so as to avoid soiling the food with droppings and bedding material. This is also advisable, since gerbils normally eat in a seated position.

Feeding while away from home

What if you need to leave home for a vacation or business trip?

Well, the fact that gerbils need very little care makes it easy for you to leave them unattended for about two days.

However, it's still wise to have someone check on them to make sure there are no accidents.
You also need to make sure that fresh bedding, dry food, and a bottle of fresh water are provided before you leave. You should also leave a chunk of raw carrot to supplement the dry food while you're gone.

Lastly, you should make sure the cage is escape-proof and positioned away from direct sunlight and draughts. If you need to be away for more than two days, then you should arrange for someone to replenish the gerbils' food and water supply as well as to change the bedding material.

Thirst

Because a gerbil's natural habitat is the desert, it doesn't require too much water. Still, you should make sure fresh water is available at all times.

Remember that gerbils love to burrow and they drink in a seated position.

This means you shouldn't place their water in a plate or bowl placed on the cage floor. Rather, you should use a watering bottle, which can easily be attached to the side of the cage with a wire clip.

Make sure your water bottle has a stainless steel spout and that the end of the spout is located a few centimetres above the top of the bedding.

Handling your gerbil

The very first time you bring your new pets home, you should provide them with food and water, but refrain from handling them for at least a day so they can rest and familiarize the surroundings. This also allows the gerbils to recover from the journey from their original home to the new one.

Once it's safe to handle them, make sure you do so by cupping your hands under their bodies before lifting them up. You should also allow the gerbil to walk around in your palm before you completely pick it up so it can get used to the experience of being in your hand. After a few minutes, you can lift it in a quick and gentle scooping motion.

Be careful not to grasp a gerbil's stomach, as that can make the animal feel trapped and therefore struggle to get out of your hand; it may even scratch you in the process.

Gerbils have an excellent sense of height and they seldom jump without giving the action some serious thought. However, it's best to hold your pet in the palm of one hand and then gently hold the base of its tail in your other hand to prevent it from accidentally falling from your hand.

You can be assured that when you place your gerbils on a table or any elevated surface, they'll understand that they shouldn't go over the edge. The risk is that they might accidentally skid off the edge or simply forget that it's there so you should take the necessary precautions.

Gerbils enjoy climbing up your arms and perching atop your shoulder, in which case you should refrain from making any sudden movements that may cause them to fall off. You may also enjoy letting them crawl in and out of your collar, pocket, or hood; just make sure you don't allow them to chew on your clothing such that they cause considerable damage.

Training

Gerbils generally bite only when they're handled badly.

For example, if you squeeze, chase, or tease your gerbil by holding your finger directly in front of its mouth, then it's likely to nip you.

If you get bitten and the bite breaks your skin, be sure to apply disinfectant.

This rule holds true regardless of what kind of pet you have. For such a small animal, a gerbil can be quite intelligent and this intelligence can be used to your advantage when taming and training your pets. What's important is for you to exercise patience and understanding to develop your pets' trust and confidence in you.

Take note that young gerbils are typically nervous and jumpy during the first few weeks of training, so it's advisable to keep your training sessions short at this time.

You should also familiarize yourself with the gerbils' activity cycle before you start training them because preventing or disrupting their rest periods can make them irritable.

During training, you need to be calm, slow, and deliberate in both your speech and movement. You have to give your pets the opportunity to get accustomed to you. Let them eat bits of lettuce or seeds from your fingers and then scratch their heads, backs, or ears gently while they're eating so they get used to your touch.

It's also a good idea to offer treats as rewards during training and as the taming and training sessions progress, you can start letting your gerbils step out of their cage and explore a larger secured area.

Gerbils normally enjoy such outings, especially if there are interesting things for them to explore in the area. You can encourage them to return to their cage after the excursion by placing some food inside. To make your gerbils happier, you could also make a playground for them. All you need for this is a large box and some toys that your gerbils prefer. You'll surely enjoy watching your gerbils play.

Never allow your gerbils to run around in your house, as they might get injured or lost.

You may allow them to explore one room in your house from time to time, though. When you do, make sure the room is escape-proof and that none of your other pets can enter. You'll also need to watch your step because gerbils love approaching human feet perhaps due to a need for physical security or because of their innate curiosity. It's okay to bring your gerbils outdoors in good weather as long as you confine them to a box or any other type of enclosure. Take note, though, that you shouldn't take your gerbils outside when they're nervous, as it can be a lot more difficult to handle them in that case.

Breeding

Gerbils in captivity breed best when you mate them in pairs. This means you shouldn't place more than one female with a single male gerbil, as this is likely to result in failure or maybe even disaster. There may be no offspring produced or worse, the females might end up bullying the male gerbil to death. Take note as well that when female gerbils lose their mate, they're typically reluctant to accept a new mate and may completely refuse a new partner.

Maturity

Gerbils become mature when they reach an age between nine and twelve weeks. Their gender generally becomes recognizable at three weeks old. A male gerbil will typically have a tapered and usually tufted bulge near the base of its tail and it'll also have a small pouch. Male gerbils are generally larger and weigh more than female gerbils.

When you place two gerbils together while they're still young, they'd usually happily pair off and when this happens, you can safely leave the male gerbil with the female gerbil at all times, even when she's nursing a litter.

Both gerbils normally take part in nest-building and they're content to build their nest using paper, leaves, or cloth.

Gerbils can breed all throughout the year and mate immediately after a litter arrives, even during the nursing period.

Their gestation period is generally 24 days and you may not notice that your female gerbil is pregnant unless you weigh her regularly. Because of their quiet nature, you may not know a litter has arrived until the newborns begin emitting their high-pitched calls. Most gerbil babies are born in the early morning or late at night, although there are also rare times when they arrive in the afternoon.

The good thing is that their birth is normally painless and uncomplicated, lasting for about an hour, regardless of the size of the litter. The female isn't likely to require help from you and it's best to leave it undisturbed during this time.
A gerbil litter normally ranges from one to ten, averaging five young gerbils. Most female gerbils bear their first litter when they reach the age of six months and about a third have their first litter at around four months. A female gerbil's reproductive life usually ends by 14 months, but for some, it can last up to 20 months.

Breeding Tips

While you're not expected to achieve the same standards and conditions set by commercial breeders, there are some things you can do to improve your chances at successfully breeding gerbils.

1. Make sure there's sufficient cage space as well as nesting and bedding material.

2. Make sure your gerbils are kept on a high-protein, low-fat diet.

3. Provide your gerbils with sufficient privacy by using a cage with one or more opaque sides.

4. Make sure there's little disturbance from household traffic and noise where the cage is located.

5. Avoid handling the gerbils in the evening.

Newborn Gerbils

Baby gerbils are pink, toothless, blind, and deaf. They're only about 5cm long and weigh just around 3g. You can leave the male gerbil with the female and its litter, as it can help keep the babies warm in their nest. The first week of a gerbil's life is critical and you should avoid handling them at this time, as that might cause the mother to smother, trample, or abandon her babies.

There are times when young gerbils stray from their nest and the mother normally brings them home by pushing them with her nose, scooping them with her forefeet, or picking them up in her mouth. She will then adjust the nest to make sure all her babies are secure and warm. In the case of large litters, the mother is likely to keep her young in two different nests and divide nursing time equally. Make sure your nursing gerbil is provided a balanced diet and adequate drinking water.

At three days old, young gerbils should already have the ability to crawl, though still in an ungainly manner. Their ears should open after five or six days and by two weeks, they should already be fully covered in fur. A few more days later, their incisors should already come through and they should start gnawing and exploring their surroundings. Their eyes should also begin to open and their movements become more coordinated by this time. At three weeks old, the young gerbils should already weigh about 14g and they should be able to start eating solid food, drinking from a water bottle, standing up, jumping, thumping their hind legs, and climbing a wire mesh.

Three weeks is also the perfect time to wean young gerbils. Although this may seem such a tender age for weaning, gerbils adjust quite easily and it's really important to remove the young from the nest at this time to avoid overcrowding in case another litter comes along.

You can choose to keep the young gerbils in a group cage until they're eight weeks old, by which time you should start caging them separately to prevent inbreeding.

The closest relationship advised for pairing gerbils off is second cousins. Remember to give each young gerbil about 130 sq cm of cage space. During the first week after weaning, the young gerbils' regular food may be combined with some unsweetened cereal. You may also offer some bread crusts soaked in milk. Make sure the water bottle's spout is positioned where the young gerbils can easily reach it.

Sometimes a litter can have one or two runts and the other gerbils may bully them. In this case, it's best to isolate the runts and allow them to grow in peace. The good news is that runts often catch up with their brothers and sisters and grow to normal size in time.

You'd be pleased to know that gerbils are relatively hardy and healthy creatures, and they typically require minimum care from their owner. Their normal life span is about two to three years. Remember that successful treatment is almost impossible where diseases of small animals are concerned.

Prevention is therefore a lot better than cure for your gerbils. This includes proper diet, adequate water, clean surroundings, sufficient ventilation and cage space, and protection against extreme temperatures. In case your gerbils suffer from intestinal disorders, be sure to check its diet. More importantly, always consult your veterinarian before treating your pet by yourself.

Finally...

Here is a handy check list to refer back to ensure a happy and healthy gerbil:

1. Try to find out about what gerbils do in the wild, so you can better understand their behaviour. This will help you keep them happy and contented while in their cage.

2. Gerbils love to bond with other gerbils. So if you can always have two gerbils. After all we all need a companion.

3. Make sure the cage you provide is big enough to give them room to run around and explore in comfort.

4. Did you know gerbils need to be let outside their cages a few times a week. This helps them keep interested and stimulates their minds. Just make sure to secure the area before letting them out, as they can squeeze through the tightest of gaps.

5. Make sure you provide them with a wheel, some structure to climb, toys to gnaw on and comfortable bedding.

6. Always ensure they get a balanced diet. Just like you they benefit from a good diet.

7. Never pull their tail.

If you follow these simple guidelines you should get great pleasure from your little gerbil companion and they should stay happy and contented.

Printed in Great Britain
by Amazon.co.uk, Ltd.,
Marston Gate.